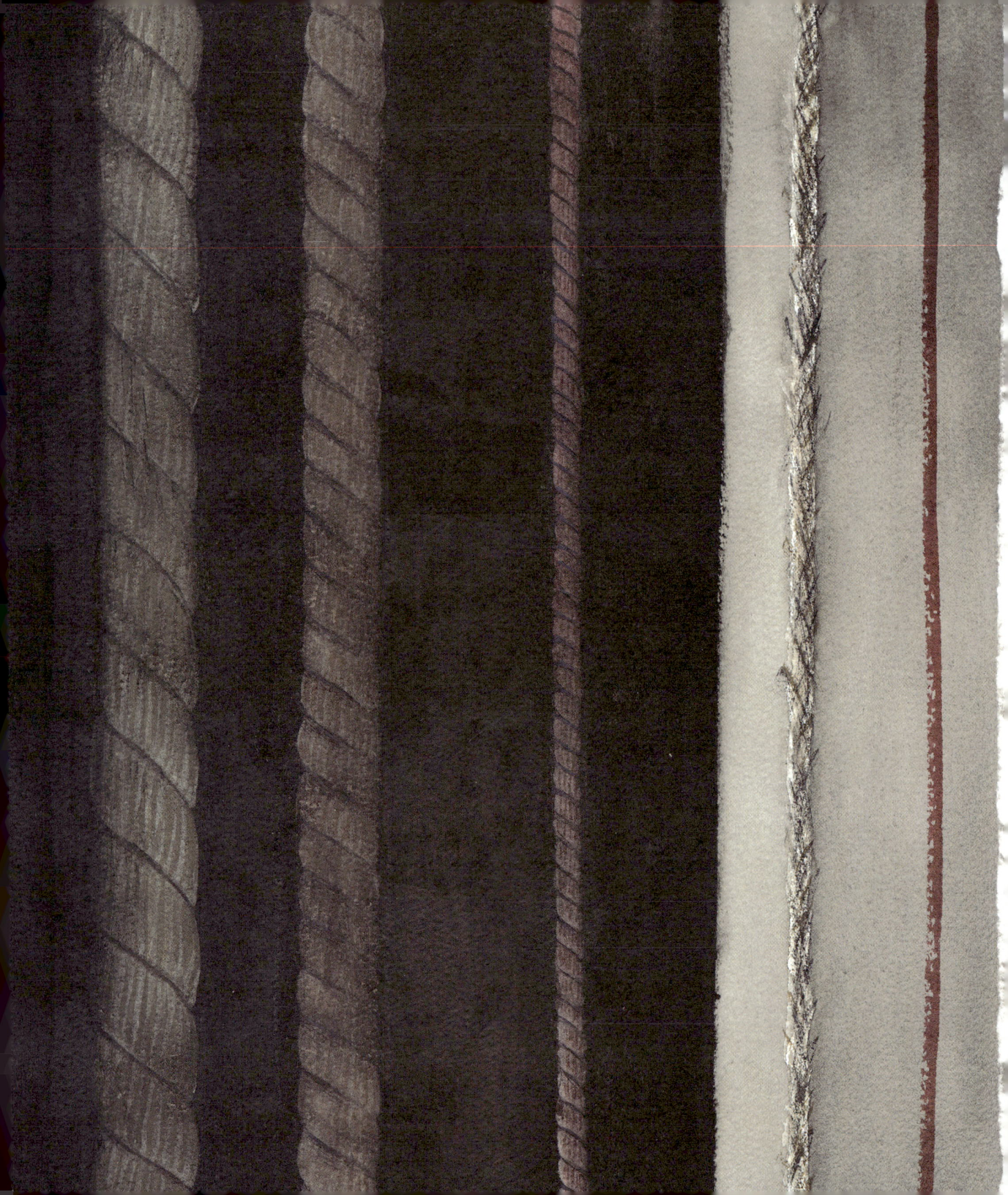

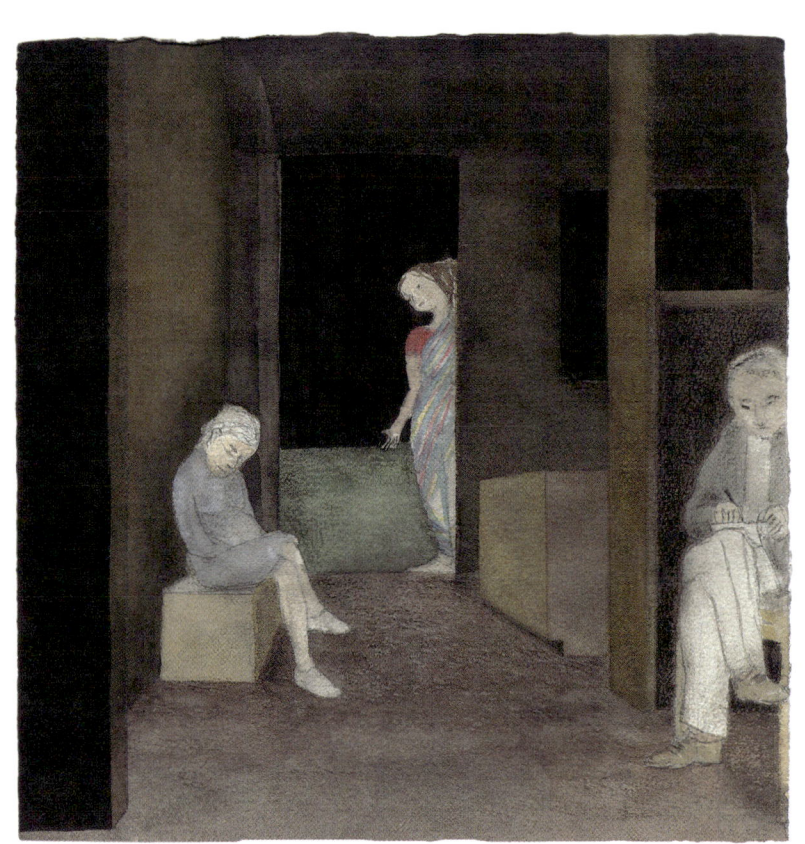

the story

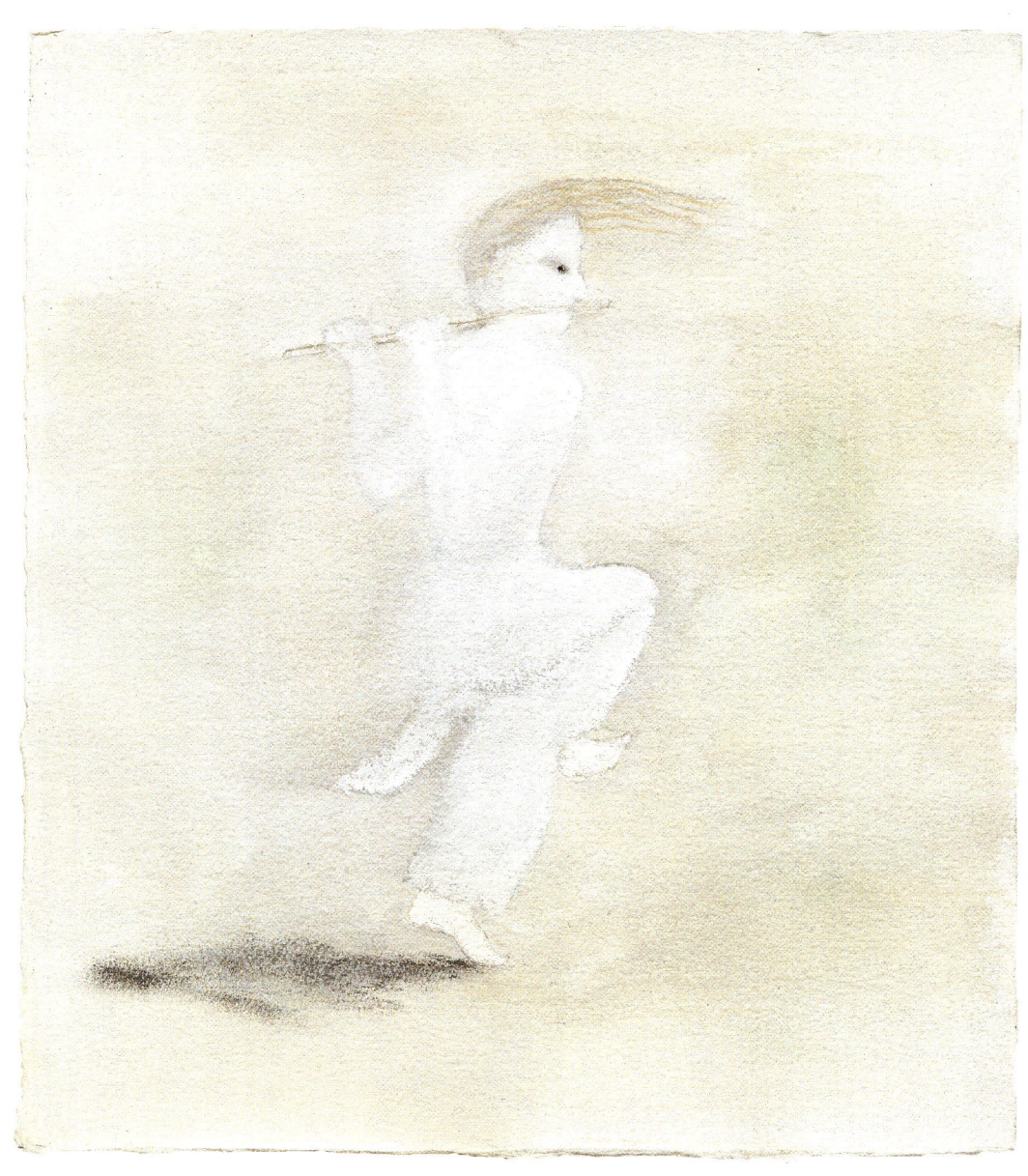

the Story

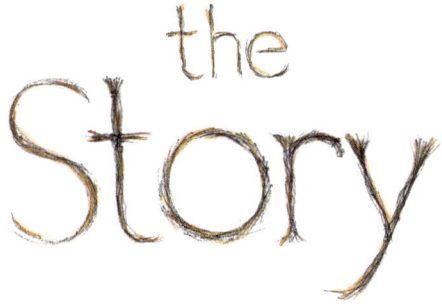

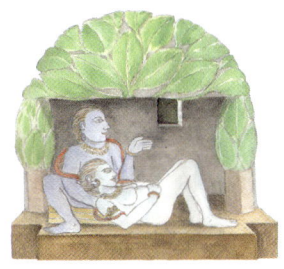

Michael Ondaatje

Drawings by David Bolduc

HOUSE OF ANANSI PRESS

"The Story" first published in Canada in 1998 in *Handwriting* by McClelland & Stewart Ltd.
First published in the United States of America in 1999 in *Handwriting* by Alfred A. Knopf.
Published in Canada in 2000 in *Handwriting* by Vintage Canada.

This edition of "The Story" published in 2005 by
House of Anansi Press Inc.
110 Spadina Avenue, Suite 801
Toronto, ON, M5V 2K4
Tel. 416-363-4343
Fax 416-363-1017
www.anansi.ca

Distributed in Canada by
HarperCollins Canada Ltd.
1995 Markham Road
Scarborough, ON, M1B 5M8
Toll free tel. 1-800-387-0117

Distributed in the United States by
Publishers Group West
1700 Fourth Street
Berkeley, CA 94710
Toll free tel. 1-800-788-3123

"The Story" is reprinted in Canada by permission of McClelland & Stewart Ltd., and by permission of Knopf Canada.
Reprinted in the United States of America by permission of Alfred A. Knopf.
"The Story" from *Handwriting*, by Michael Ondaatje. New York: Alfred A. Knopf, 1999.

09 08 07 06 05   1 2 3 4 5

Library and Archives Canada Cataloguing in Publication Data

Ondaatje, Michael, 1943–
The story / Michael Ondaatje ; drawings by David Bolduc.

A poem.
ISBN 0-88784-194-5

1. Mother and infant — Poetry. I. Bolduc, David, 1945– II. Title.

PS8529.N283S76 2005   C811'.54   C2005-904103-X

Text design and typesetting: Stan Bevington

We acknowledge for their financial support of our publishing program
the Canada Council for the Arts, the Ontario Arts Council, and the Government of Canada
through the Book Publishing Industry Development Program (BPIDP).

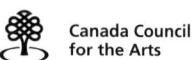

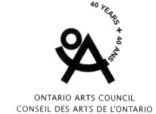

Printed and bound in China

"The Story" is for Akash and Mrs Mishra

the story

i

For his first forty days a child

is given dreams of previous lives.

Journeys, winding paths,

a hundred small lessons

and then the past is erased.

Some are born screaming,

some full of introspective wandering

into the past – that bus ride in winter,

the sudden arrival within

a new city in the dark.

And those departures from family bonds

leaving what was lost and needed.

So the child's face is a lake

of fast moving clouds and emotions.

A last chance for the clear history of the self.

All our mothers and grandparents here,

our dismantled childhoods

in the buildings of the past.

Some great forty-day daydream

before we bury the maps.

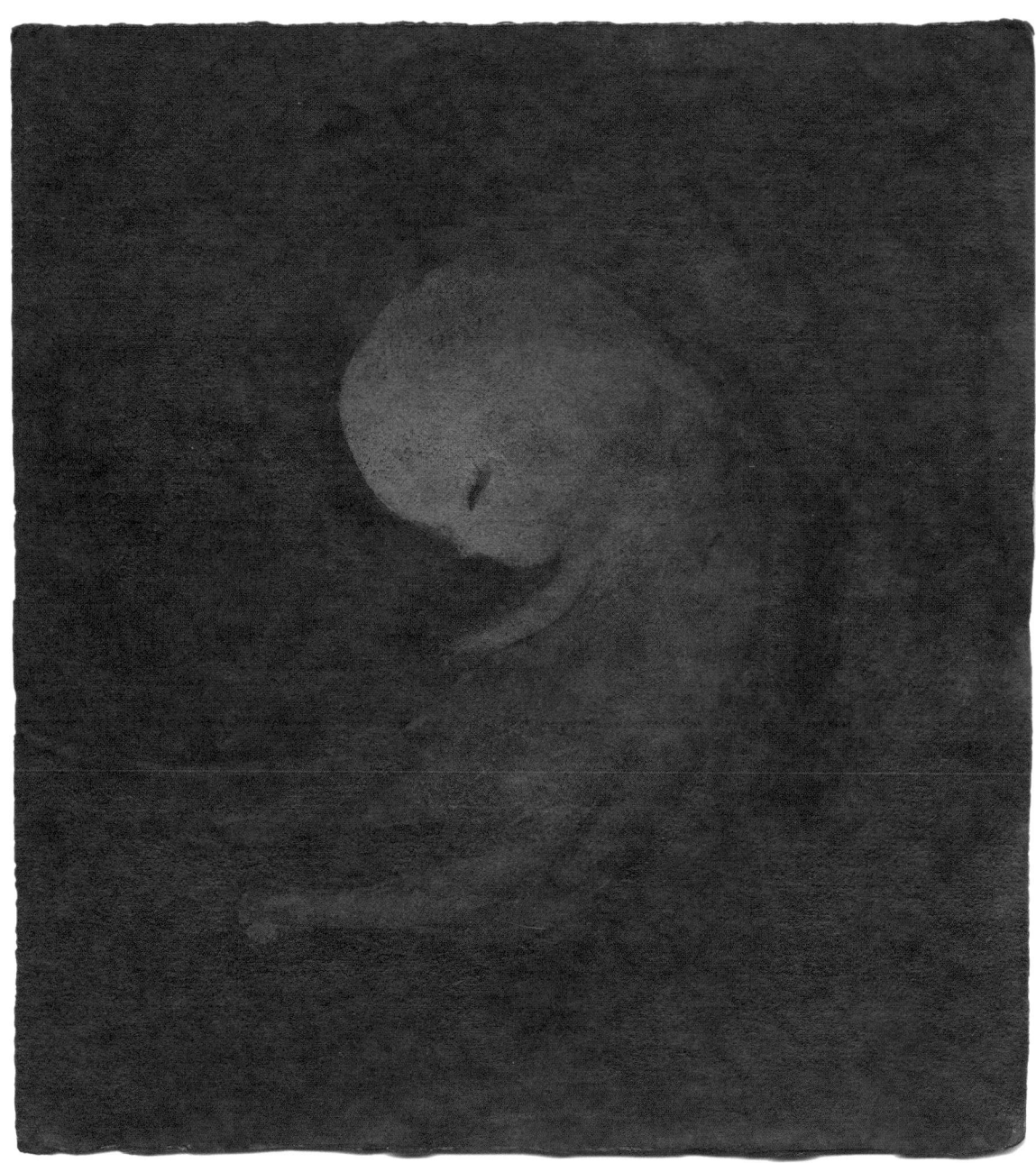

ii

There will be a war, the king told his pregnant wife.

In the last phase seven of us will cross

the river to the east and disguise ourselves

through the farmlands.

We will approach the markets

and befriend the rope-makers. Remember this.

She nods and strokes the baby in her belly.

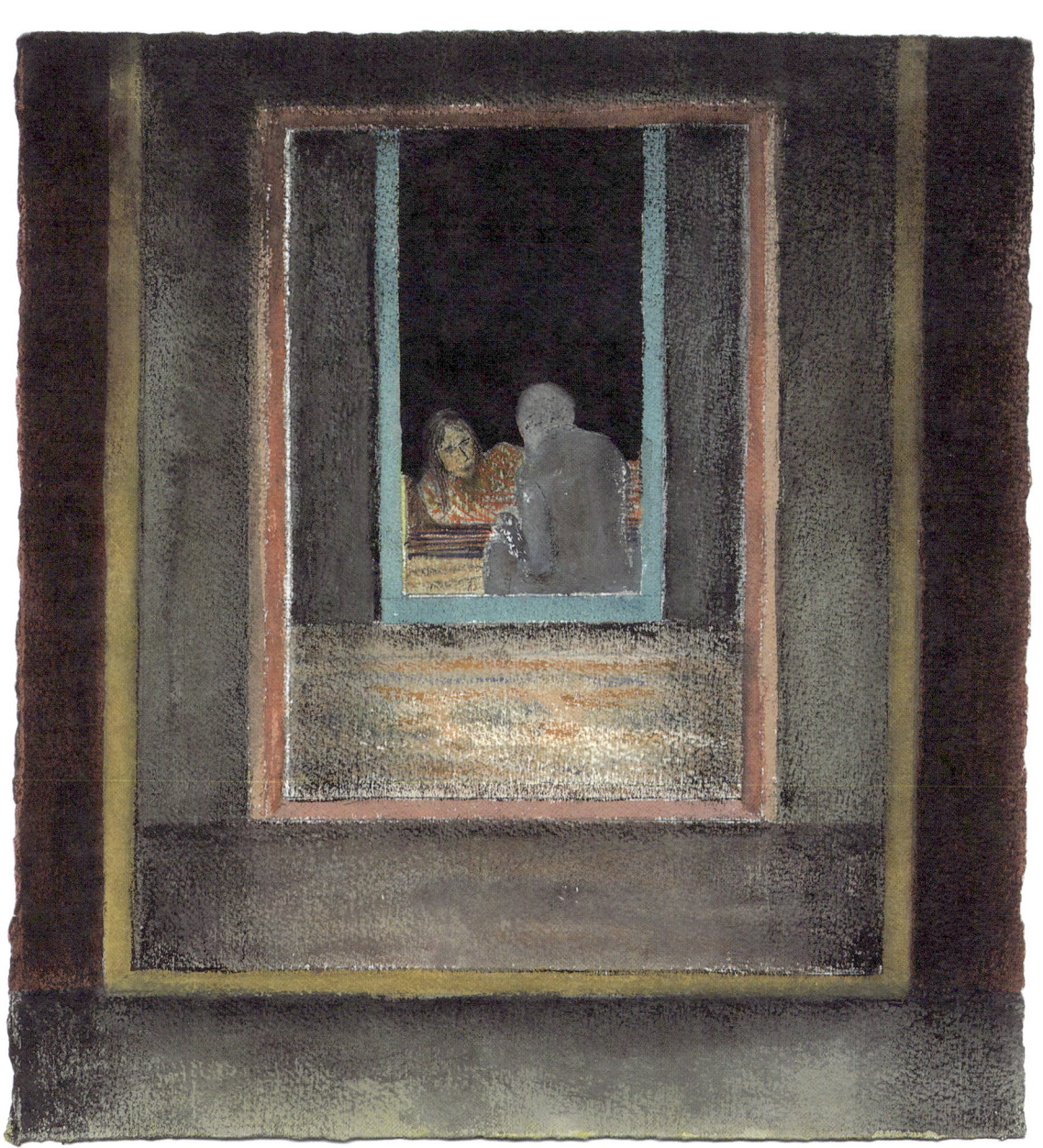

After a month we will enter

the halls of that king.

There is dim light from small high windows.

We have entered with no weapons,

just rope in the baskets.

We have trained for years

to move in silence, invisible,

not one creak of bone,

not one breath,

even in lit rooms,

in order to disappear into this building

where the guards live in half-light.

When a certain night falls

the seven must enter the horizontal door

remember this, face down,

as in birth.

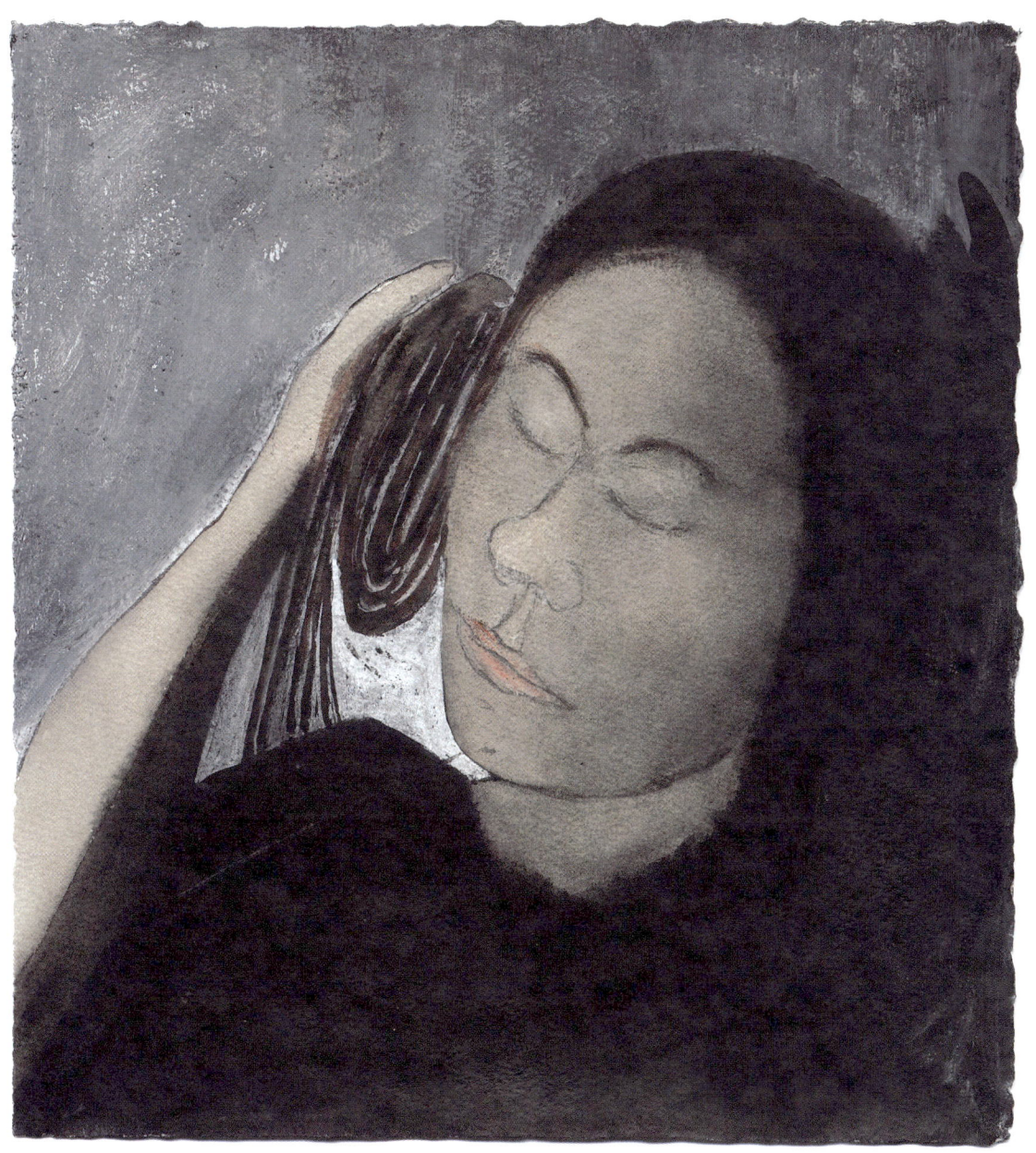

Then (he tells his wife)

there is the corridor of dripping water,

a noisy rain, a sense

of creatures at your feet.

And we enter halls of further darkness,

cold and wet among the enemy warriors.

To overcome them we douse the last light.

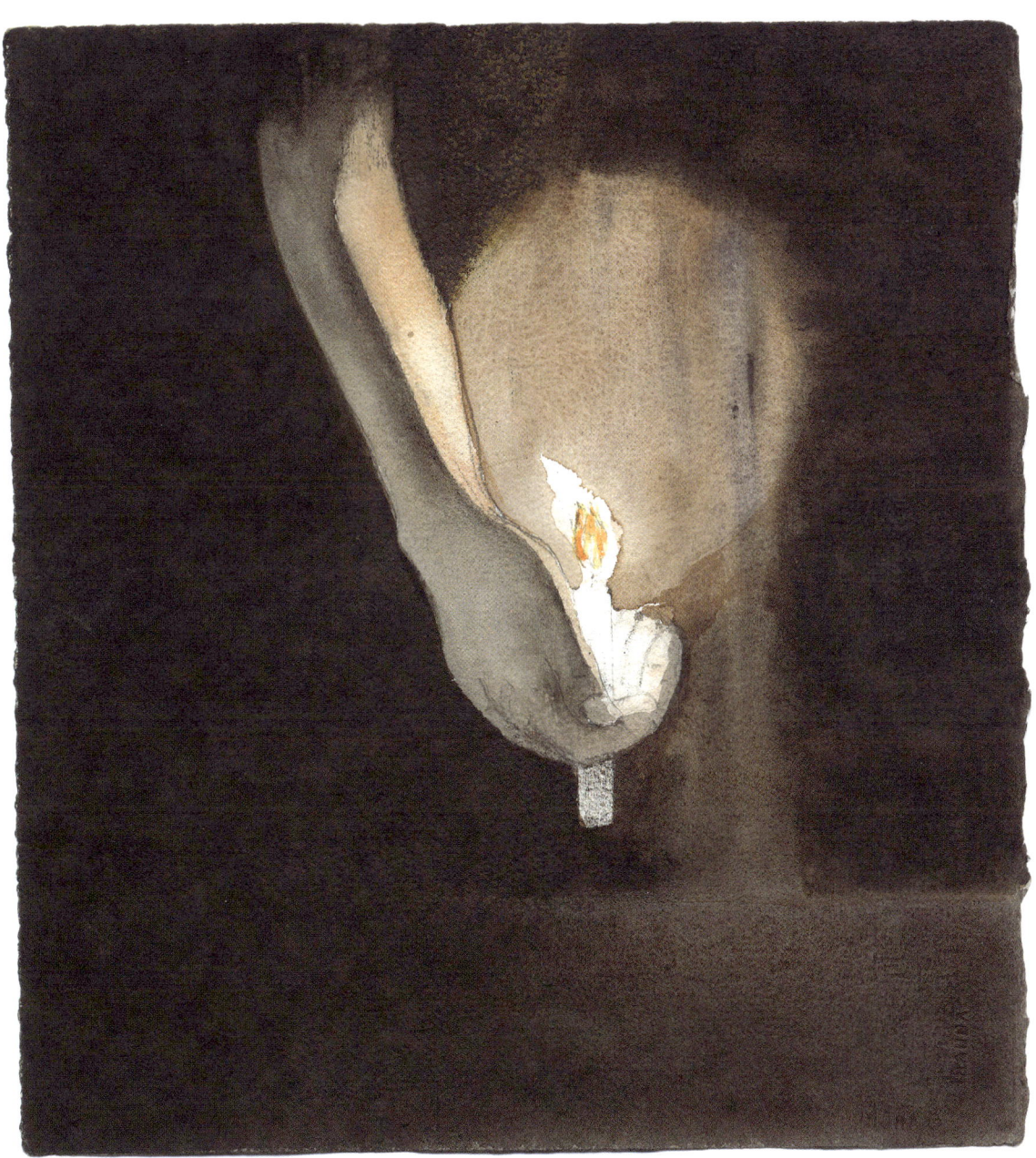

After battle we must leave another way

avoiding all doors to the north . . .

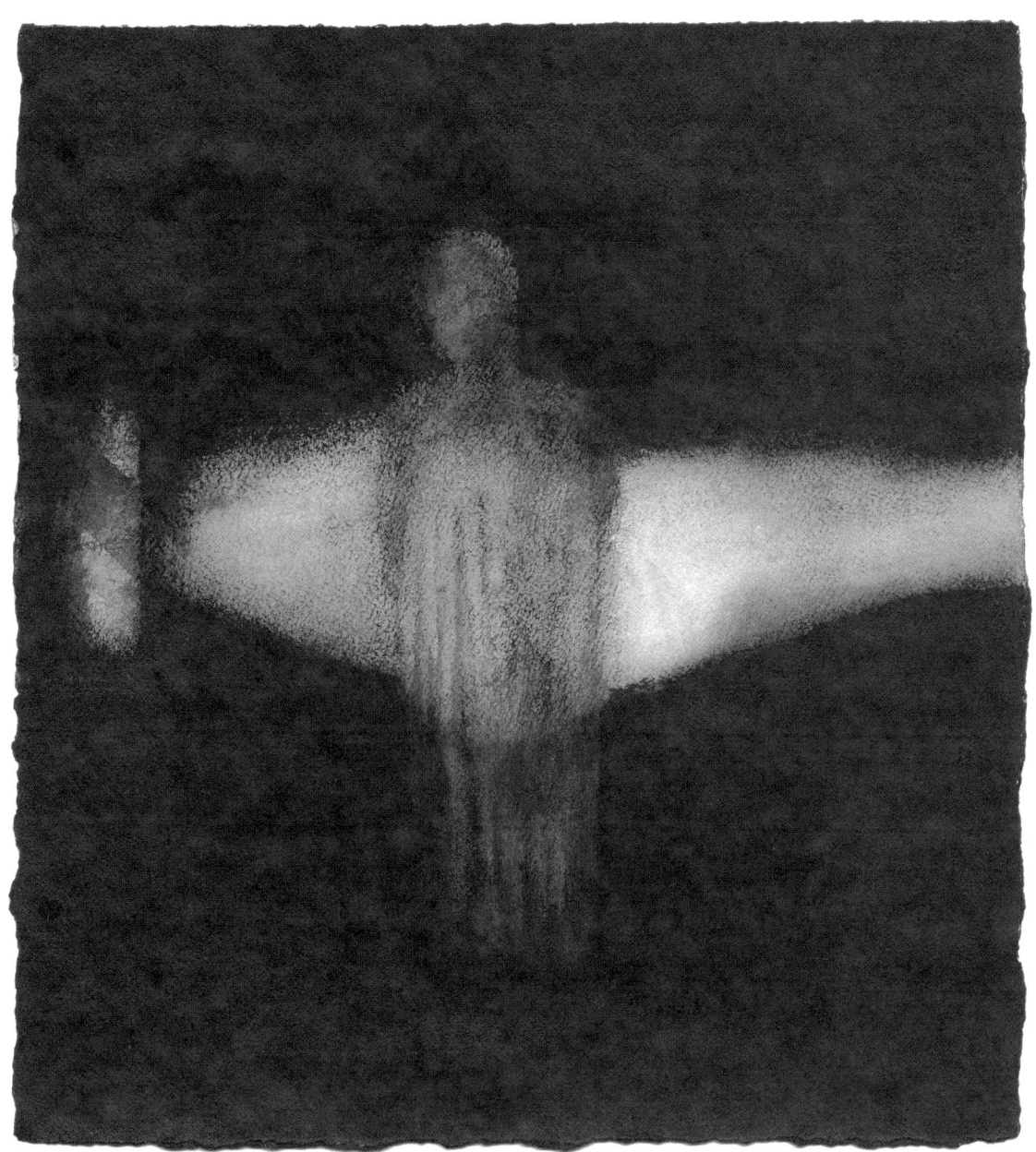

(The king looks down

and sees his wife is asleep

in the middle of the adventure.

He bends down and kisses through the skin

the child in the body of his wife.

Both of them in dreams. He lies there,

watches her face as it catches a breath.

He pulls back a wisp across her eye

and bites it off. Braids it

into his own hair, then sleeps beside them.)

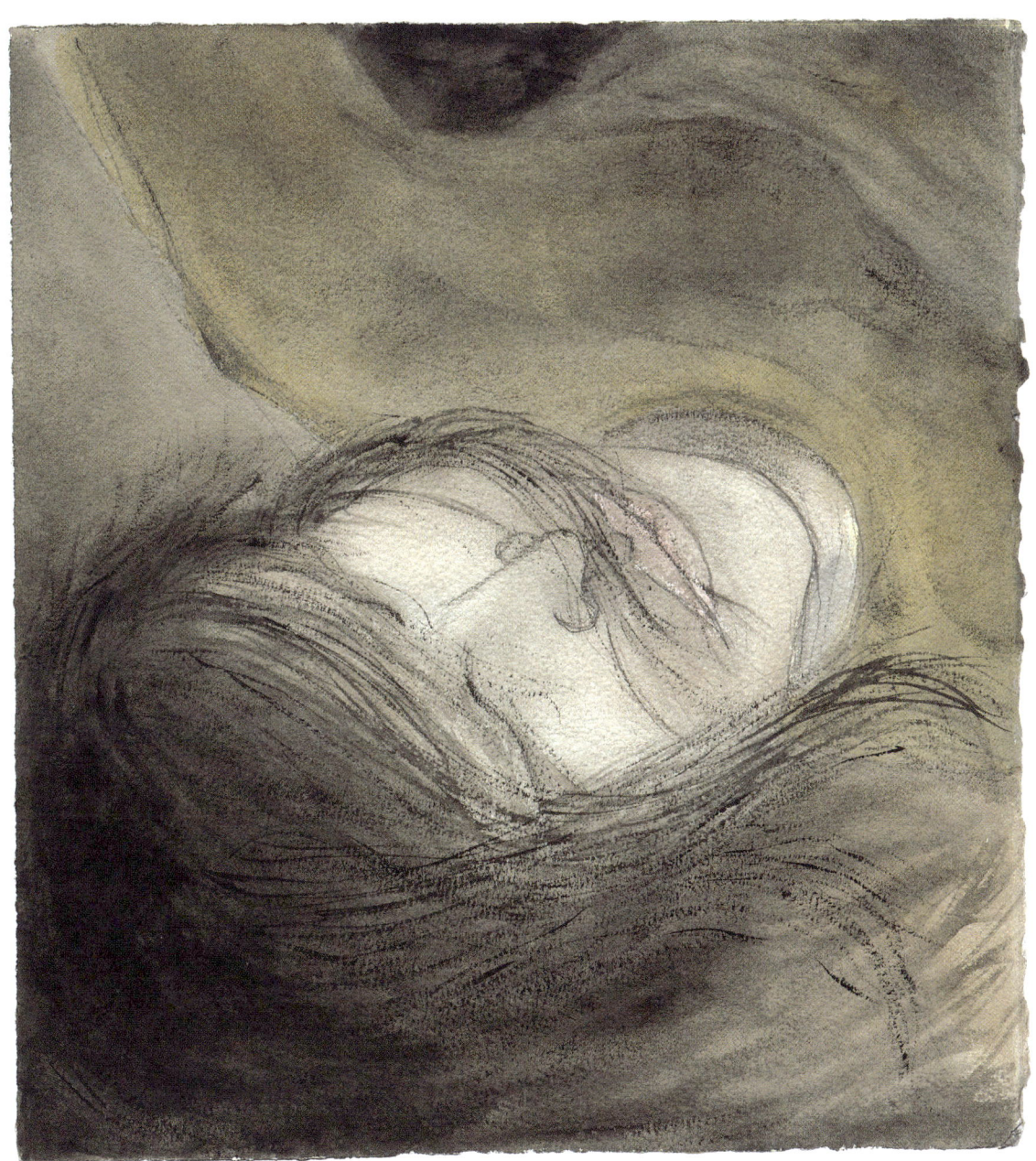

iii

With all the swerves of history

I cannot imagine your future.

Would wish to dream it, see you

in your teens, as I saw my son,

your already philosophical air

rubbing against the speed of the city.

I no longer guess a future.

And do not know how we end

nor where.

Though I know a story about maps, for you.

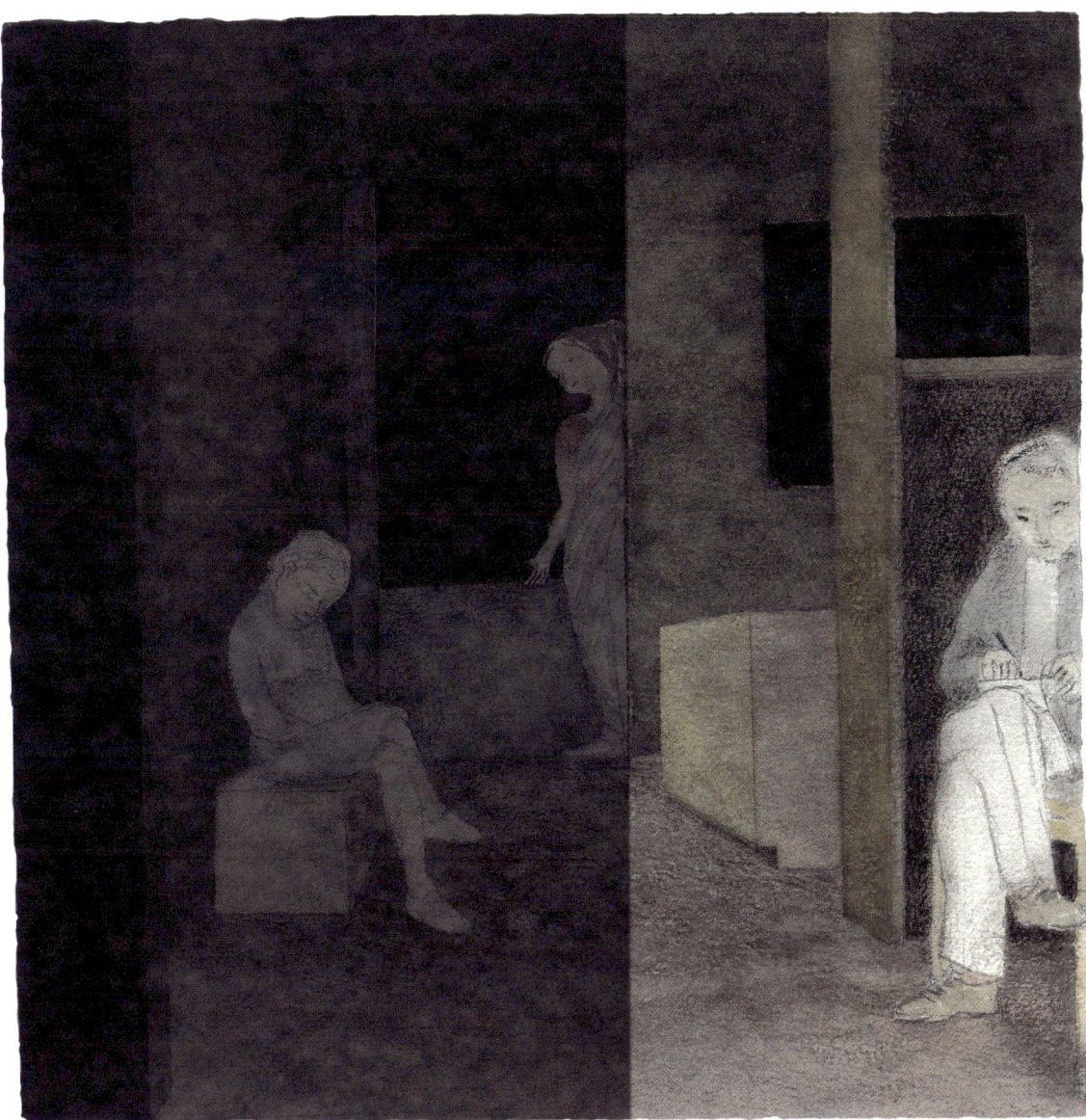

iv

After the death of his father,

the prince leads his warriors

into another country.

Four men and three women.

They disguise themselves and travel

through farms, fields of turnip.

They are private and shy

in an unknown, uncaught way.

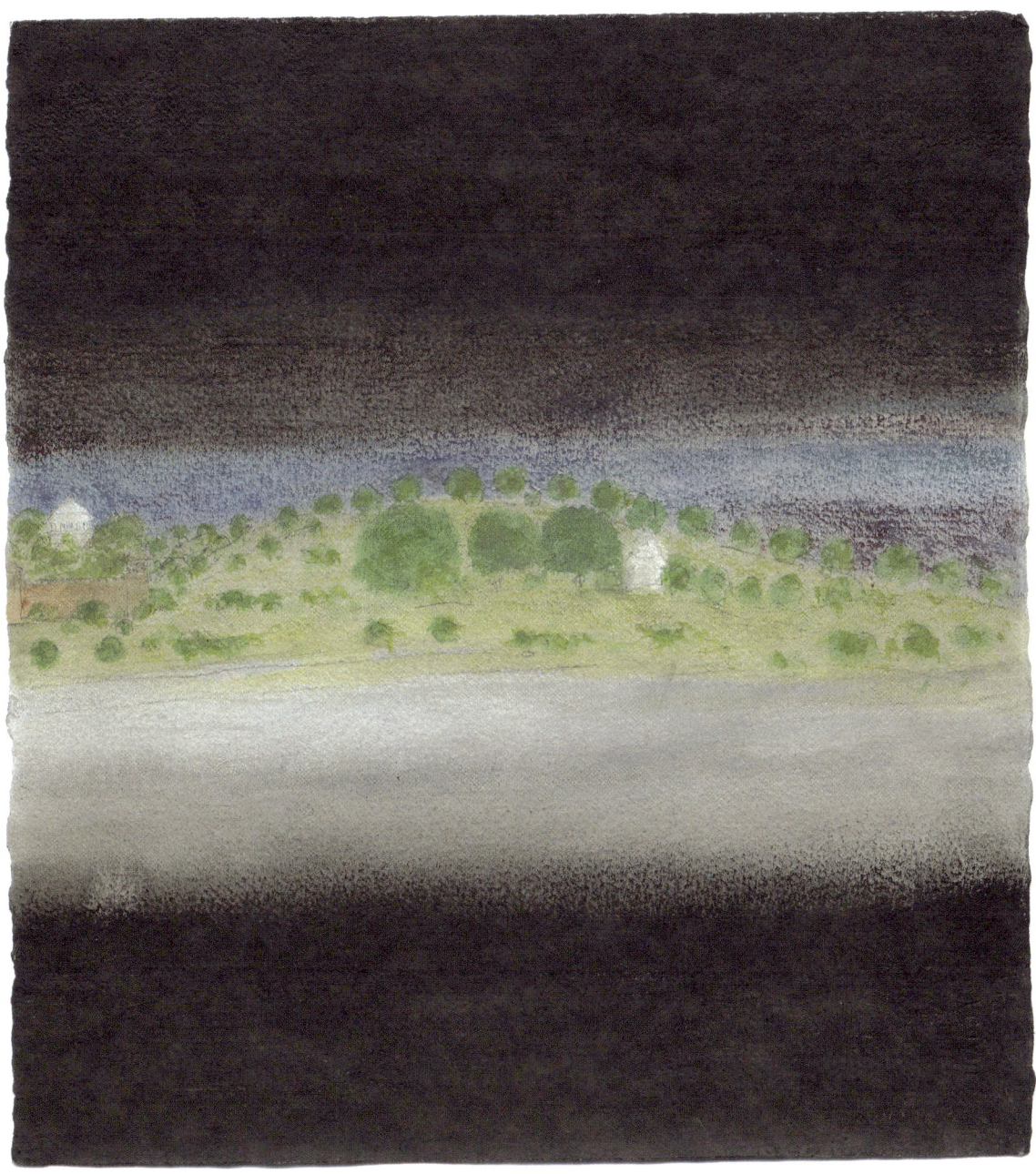

In the hemp markets

In the hemp markets

they court friends.

They court friends.

They are dancers who tumble

They are dancers who tumble

with lightness as they move,

with lightness as they move,

their long hair wild in the air.

their long hair wild in the air.

Their shyness slips away.

Their shyness slips away.

They are charming with desire in them.

They are charming with desire in them.

It is the dancing they are known for.

It is the dancing they are known for.

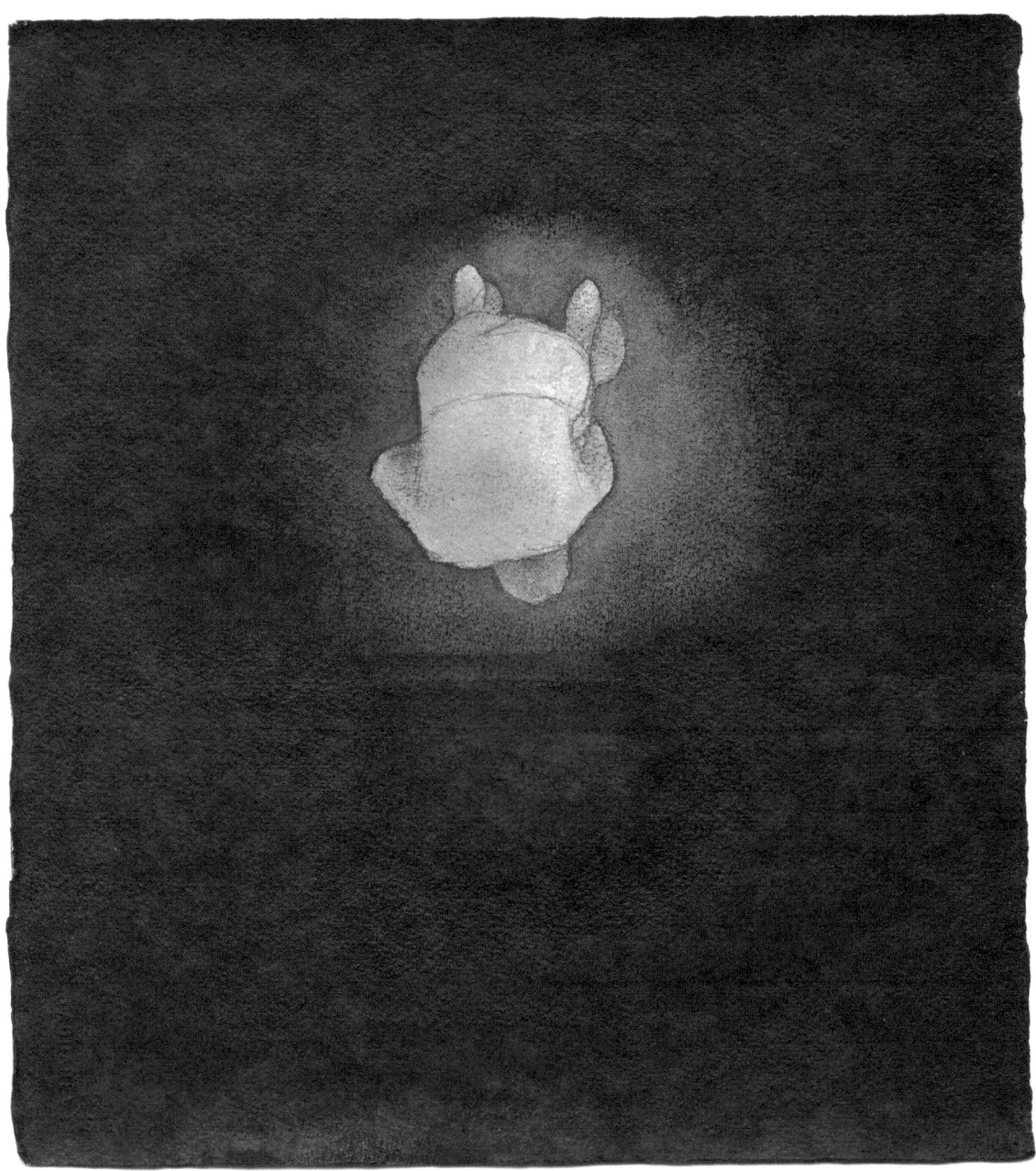

One night they leave their beds.

Four men, three women.

They cross open fields where nothing grows

and swim across the cold rivers

into the city.

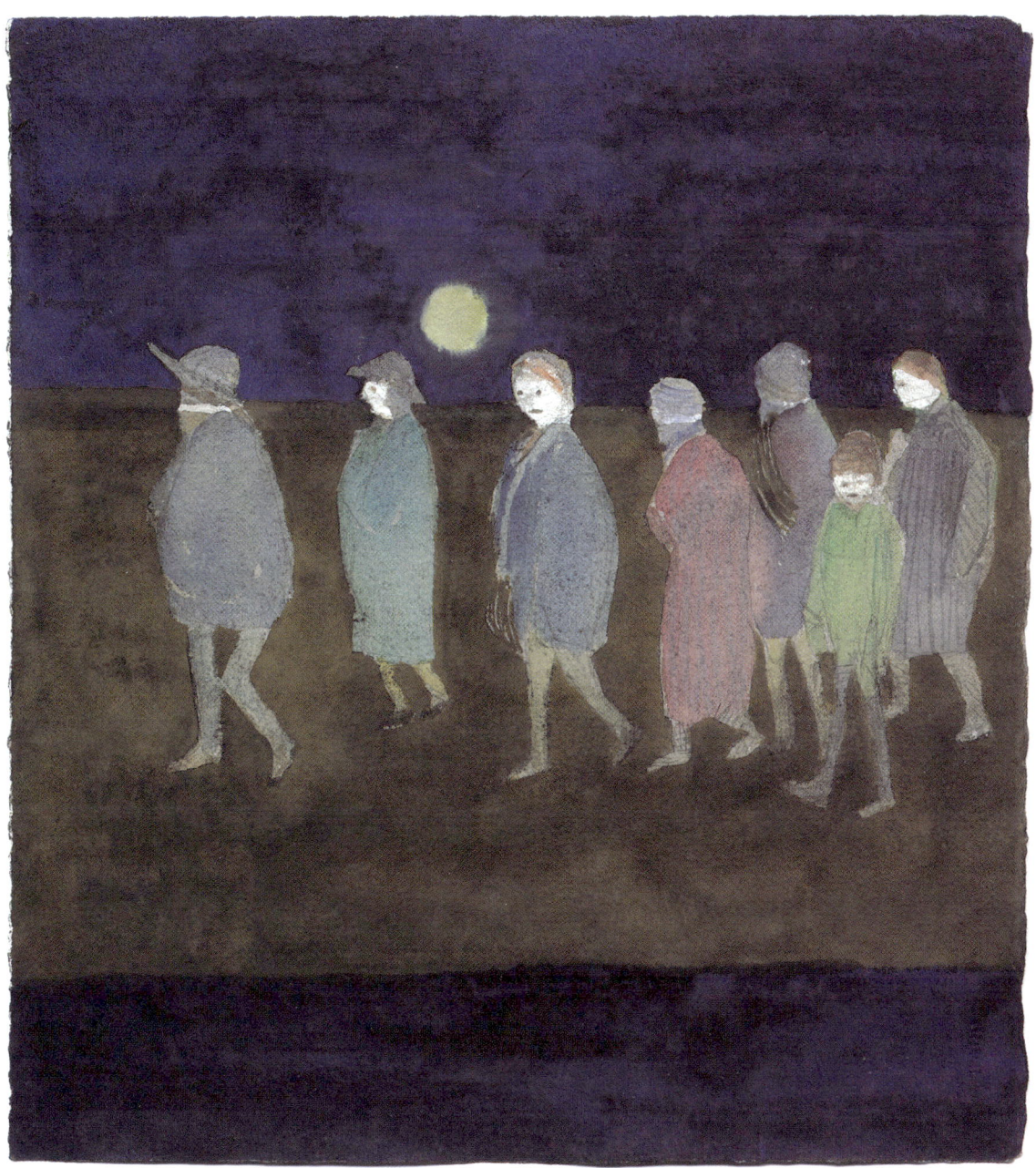

Silent, invisible among the guards,

they enter the horizontal door

face down so the blades of poison

do not touch them. Then

into the rain of the tunnels.

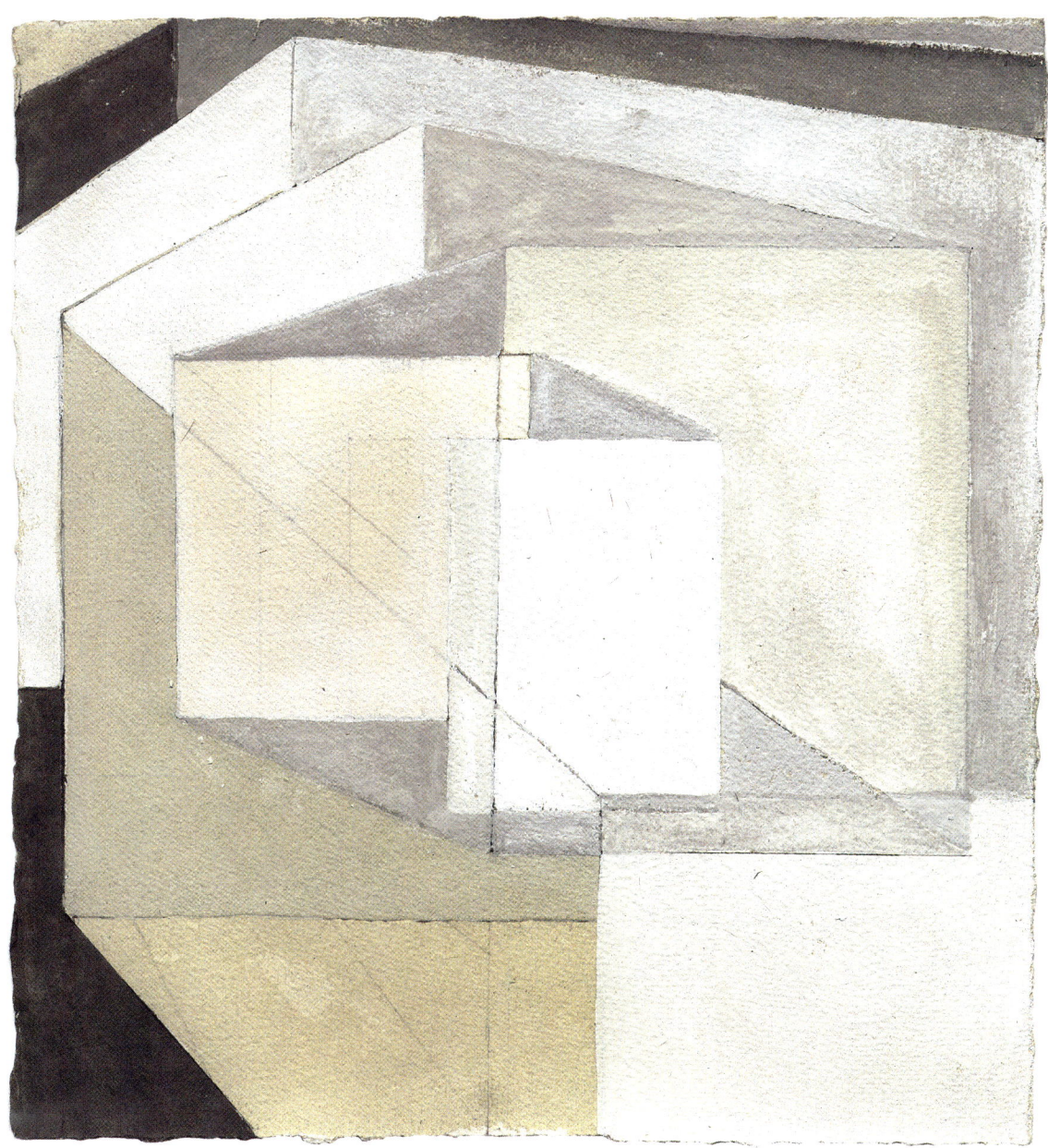

It is an old story – that one of them

remembers the path in.

They enter the last room of faint light

and douse the lamp. They move

within the darkness like dancers

at the centre of a maze

seeing the enemy before them

with the unlit habit of their journey.

There is no way to behave after victory.

*

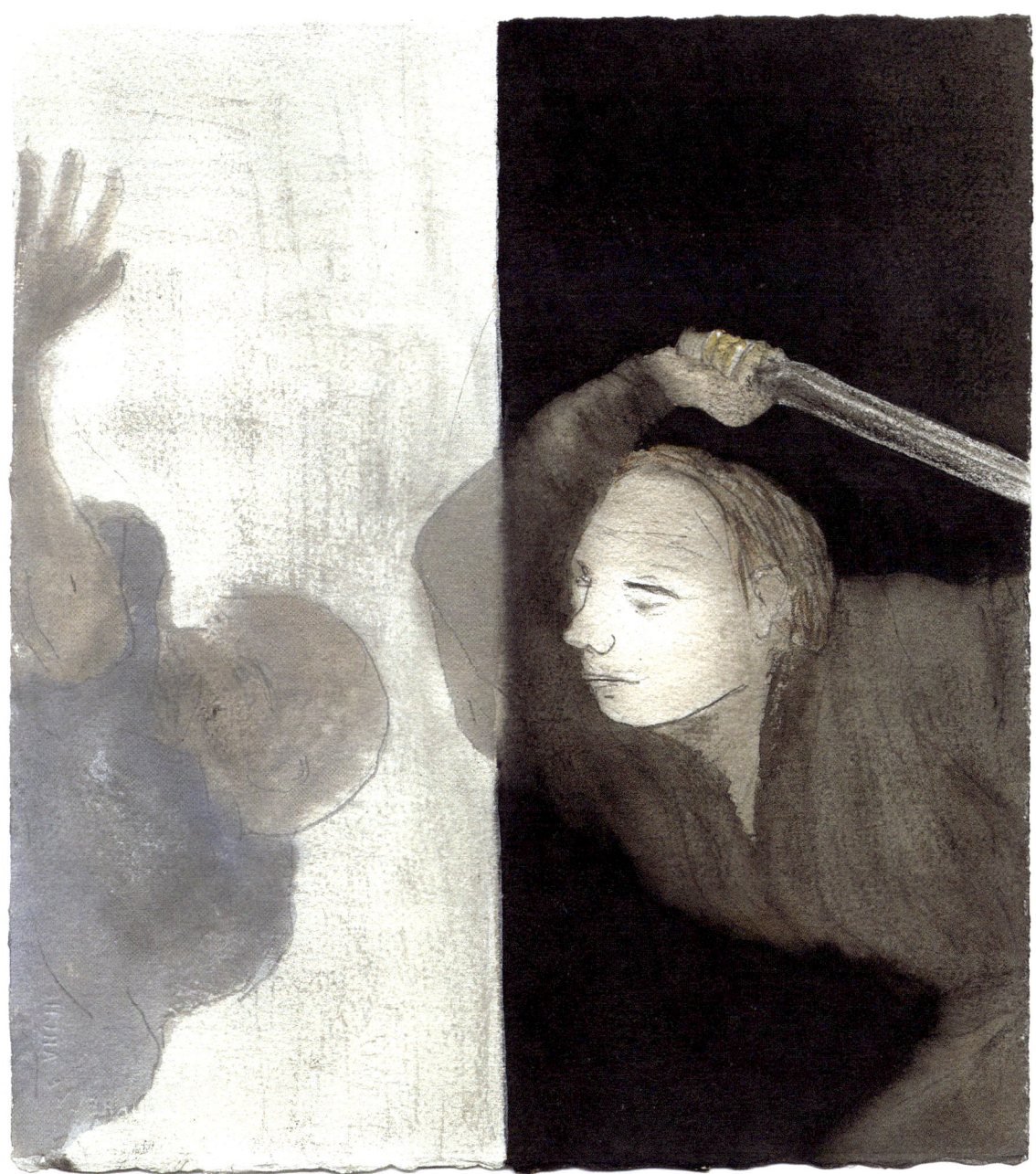

And what should occur now is unremembered.

The seven stand there.

One among them, who was that baby,

cannot recall the rest of the story

– the story his father knew, unfinished

that night, his mother sleeping.

We remember it as a tender story,

though perhaps they perish.

The father's lean arm across

the child's shape, the taste

of the wisp of hair in his mouth . . .

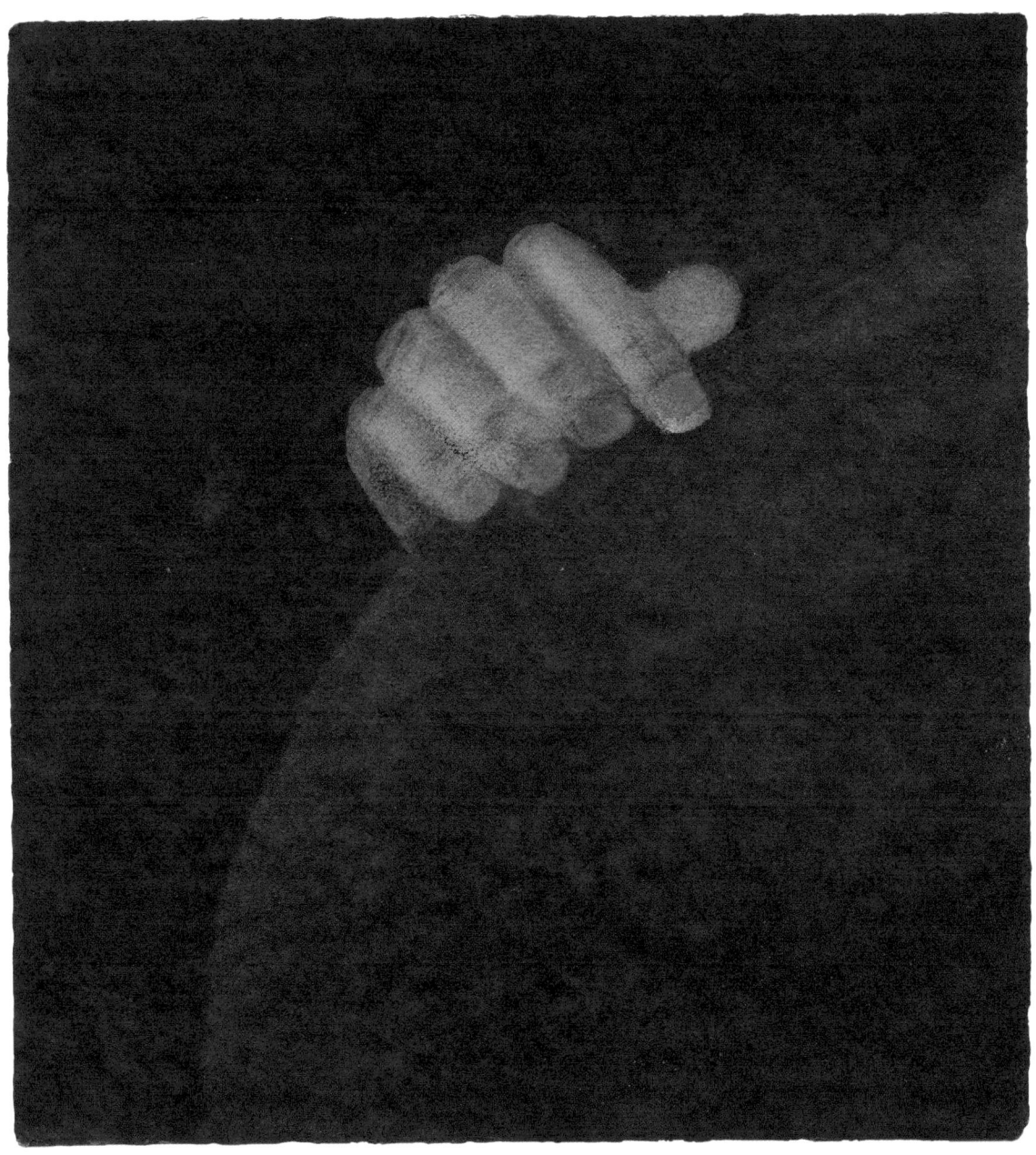

The seven embrace in the destroyed room

where they will die without

the dream of exit.

We do not know what happened.

From the high windows the ropes

are not long enough to reach the ground.

They take up the knives of the enemy

and cut their long hair and braid it

onto one rope and they descend

hoping it will be long enough

into the darkness of the night.

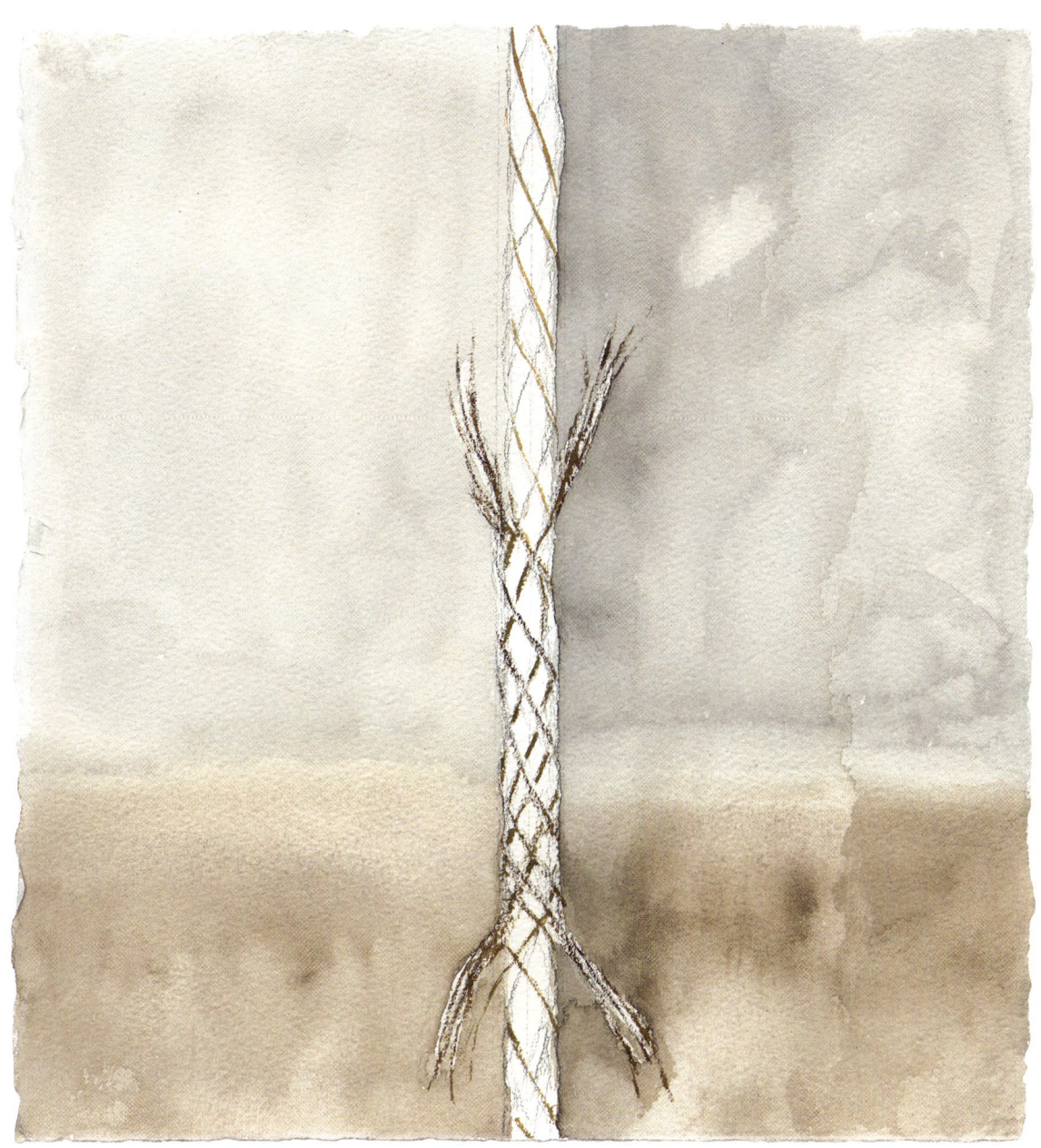

This book was first printed in a special limited edition to celebrate the fiftieth anniversary of the founding of World Literacy of Canada.

Freedom, empowerment, opportunity, and hope are what World Literacy of Canada is all about. We believe that reading and writing are fundamental to the creation of a better world where knowledge and power are more equally shared.

World Literacy of Canada's programs include women's literacy classes, tutoring and scholarships for children, income generation projects, community health advocacy, and development of small local libraries. All royalties from the sale of this book will support these programs.

For more on World Literacy of Canada, please contact us at:
401 Richmond Street West, Studio 236, Toronto, Ontario, Canada, M5V 3A8
Telephone: 416.977.0008   Website: www.worldlit.ca   Email: info@worldlit.ca

.

ACKNOWLEDGEMENTS

World Literacy of Canada is grateful to Michael Ondaatje, David Bolduc, Scott Griffin, and Ed Burtynsky for their kind generosity. Thanks to House of Anansi Press, Coach House Press, Toronto Image Works, Atelier GF, and McClelland & Stewart Ltd., and to Jeannie Baxter, Erik Syberland, Bazil Abbasi, Susan Farquhar, Robert Game, Sarah MacLachlan, Martha Sharpe, Kevin Linder, and Jason McBride for their valuable support. "The Story" from *Handwriting* by Michael Ondaatje is reprinted in Canada by permission of McClelland & Stewart Ltd. and in the United States of America by permission of Alfred A. Knopf.

COLOPHON

The text was designed by Stan Bevington and set into type
at the Coach House Press on bpNichol Lane, Toronto.
The book was first printed in a limited edition of 125 numbered copies
by the Coach House Press.

The text typeface is Cartier Book, designed and digitized by Rod Mcdonald
based on a 1967 Canadian font by Carl Dair.